Pithy Cakes

Also by Jill Loree

Spilling the Script
An Intense Guide to Self-Knowing
www.phoenesse.org

The Guide Speaks
—The Complete Q&A Collection—
By Eva Pierrakos with Jill Loree
www.theguidespeaks.org

Pithy Cakes

Quippy Confections About
Making it Through

Jill Loree

Published by Phoenesse LLC
Discover more from Jill Loree at www.phoenesse.com.

ISBN-10: 1516962923
ISBN-13: 978-1516962921

Photo of Paul Bunyan and Babe the Blue Ox, mythical characters of legendary size credited with creating the Finger Lakes (apparently Paul had very large hands) as well as the many lakes dotting the upper Midwest (Babe, it seems, had very large feet), courtesy of Mark Fairchild, Associate Dean of Research & Graduate Education, and Professor & Program Director of the Color Science/Munsell Color Science Laboratory at Rochester Institute of Technology, College of Science.

Dedication

Well, we got trouble my friends, right here in River City. That's a capital T and that rhymes with P and that stands for....Pithy. Somehow that worked out better for the Music Man. True fact, this book is being brought to you by the letter T. As in Trust. It has taken me a boatload of trust to get to the place I find myself today, and all I can say is: I am just so glad to be finding myself.

I am grateful for every single dropperful of trust I have been able to muster over the past year or two. I am also thankful for the love of my family, and most especially for the unwavering support from my two sons. Charlie and Jackson, this one's for you.

    – Jill Loree

Contents

Changing Gears

I once had a friend who drove a stick, and on our way to lunch one day, I noticed she had problems getting into second gear. This was caused by her habit of revving the engine coming out of first gear and just skipping into third. After bypassing second gear for so long, she later couldn't find it when she wanted it—or needed it.

It seems this past year of my life has been about learning to work with those lower gears. I left a good job in the city where the big wheels were always turning. Working fulltime while doing things like getting two kids to soccer practice, working on my spiritual path, serving as president of a homeowner's association when big zoning issues were hitting the fan, and taking care of the house. You get the idea. I needed to have my tuckus in gear at all times to get 'er done.

I did my best to take time out to relax, read the paper, enjoy some live theater, or go for a run—oh wait, that last one actually came off the to-do list. My point is, I didn't have much time to spend in second gear, but at least I made a short pause there on my way past it.

And then my whole life shifted into this whole new slowed-down mode. I am in the process of making an intentional major turn toward a new destination, but I can't yet see around the corner. So I find myself waiting, and preparing, and not worrying, and preparing some more, and trying really hard not to worry, and having more space than I know what to do with. It has sort of been exhausting, getting used to this.

I am reminded of this quote from Andrew Jackson: "I was born for the storm, and a calm does not suit me." Lately, I feel like a finely-tuned sports car that is now meandering through a cozy neighborhood, trying not to speed in the school zone. Also trying not to rev my engine at stop signs, or peal out and leave rubber behind me. You can't go fast enough here for third gear without getting a $425 ticket. Trust me, I know about these things.

What I've been learning about lately is what it really means to trust. I have come to know that I can trust myself. But how about God? Can I trust, even when my ego-brain is not convinced this is a good idea? This, I think, is where the rubber meets the road.

Can I find that place in my gut where I know that all is well? Do I trust that God knows what he's doing? Can I look at the level of trust that is being called forth in me and see the divinity in this very plan?

I've done a lot of work to get here. This isn't about being irresponsible or out of touch. In fact, I'm in touch all day long with the inner source that guides me and is leading me to where I am ready to go.

I can hear the gentle hum of the engine, but I seem to be idling—not in any gear. It's like I'm sitting at some type of crossroads wondering if I am to go right or left. Actually, I do know. They say, When nothings goes right, go left. Blinker is on.

A little missive sent to friends and family on New Year's Eve 2013; six months later, even my address changed.

Rhymes with "New Me!"

My email changed, my number changed,
(My address stayed the same,)
My goodness, why not go ahead
And change up my last name?

For twenty years it's been the same
As my two awesome boys,
Who now are nearly grown up men—
My dear sweet pride-and-joys.

But it's been over ten years now
That I've been on my own,
And now it's time to make this change
To set a whole new tone.

So now my middle name will be
My last, officially.
I'm pleased to introduce to you,
My new self, Jill Loree!

Pithy Cakes

It's Like Being Psychic

I did one of those whole-house updates a few years back, the kind where you look at everything, literally, and if you don't love it, you pitch it. It was a real barn burner, that one. During the entire process, I was tuning in deeply to what worked—in my house, but more importantly, in my gut—and I developed a really good feel for it. I also made a lot of trips back-and-forth to the store.

Around that time, I was also feeling into—sounds new-agey doesn't it, "feeling into"—how things would go, both in this house project and the multitude of projects I had going on at work. I was developing a sense for when something was "ripe."

In other words, to know when it was time to move on something, and when it just wasn't quite time yet. And more than that, I started to tune into how I thought a project would go. You know, this one isn't going to be that big a deal, or there is something snakebit about this one but I don't know what it is.

I recall one little project, which was to replace the fixtures in my half-bath. I had gone through the steps of selecting and picking up everything I needed, including the faucet, towel rack and toilet paper holder. A plumber had installed the faucet, but there the rack and holder sat, hanging up in my gut every time I thought about installing them. I can work a drill and a screwdriver just fine, so this didn't make sense, the tiny feeling of dread. So I kept sitting with it, noticing it.

Finally, push came to shove and it was time to get this one done. I decided to just go slowly and pay close attention. I got to the part where you insert the little set screw that tightens the towel holder into place, and wouldn't you know, it would not fit. It was flat out the wrong size. And of the mishmash of set screws I had in my toolbox, none were the right size. Two trips to Home Depot later—I don't even recall now why the first replacement also didn't work—the job was done. And that's when I knew why the hang-up in my gut.

I remember telling my healer about how I was having experiences like this left, right and center, and saying, "It's sort of like being psychic." And she said, "Actually, that *is* being psychic." OK, now that sounds really new-agey.

Here's the thing. I have come to see that this ability to tune into my own gut—and to cut my teeth doing it on projects as trivial as a towel holder—is huge. To develop trust by way of the droplets of everyday-minutia, has given me a bucket full of courage to take the steps I have taken this past year.

Because when it comes time to listen deeply to an inner voice that says it'll be OK to quit your job, sell your house and move half-way across the country to a place you've barely visited, you better have something more to rely on than the ability to follow a hunch.

I used to think that psychics were all about predicting the future. I now think there is more value in being able to hear the small, quiet voice of the present. The one that says "stay here, stay here, stay here." I'll know when the time is ripe to move ahead.

Intense Mindfulness

Orange sherbet sunrise
Calms my heart and stills my thoughts.
Ah, my brain freezes.

Pithy Cakes

Turning Vintage into Fine

A few years back, I dated a guy who worked in wealth management, who often asked his friends and wealthy clients, "What's been your favorite decade, so far?" Invariably, they all said their fifties.

There were basically three reasons they gave for this. First, their children were all grown. Second, their health was still pretty good. And third, they had come to realize that this was about how far they would go—in their career, or basically in life. In other words, they could stop "striving." Check, check, check. I get that.

Now, in my early fifties, after a couple decades of working on myself, I no longer feel in need of any kind of fix. I'm not broken. Sure, I had some work to do. But as I have emerged on the other side of the renovation, I feel good-as-new. In fact, I'm really better than I have ever been.

So then just when a person's getting their sea legs in life, a funny thing happens. Wrinkles. Yeah, really funny things, these wrinkles. Like lines on a map showing how far you've come, they are a telltale sign that you've got some miles under your belt.

One thing I have noticed is that without the aid of a mirror, I can't actually see them myself. At least not the ones on my face or neck. So the only way I know they are there is by looking at what gets reflected back to me.

9

And as I have come to realize, all the world's really just a mirror.

The other thing I realize is that they really aren't hurting a thing. I mean, it's not like they actually hurt. I guess it could be a problem if they, like, got caught in a zipper. But so far, I've been good on that front.

At the same time, I have noticed that people in my age group—really anyone over about 40—is likely to need reading glasses to see fine details up close. So the closer you get, the blurrier the focus. Well now, isn't that a crazy coincidence?

So what do we think, total accident of creation—like maybe God somehow forgot to put in a prescription renewal for elastin? Or is there something deeper happening here, behind the lines, so to speak. But just what is it they are trying to tell us?

Clearly, they are not an oracle that reveals whether a person has something insightful to say. So when you're hoping for wisdom, they can often give a false positive. On the other hand, how else would we know where we might find a treasure? How else might we guess there's a greater depth to be plumbed? Isn't it the patina that makes an antique valuable? Isn't it the distortion in old windows that adds charm? Isn't it the vintage of the wine that tells of quality?

I suppose it's like looking at used cars: after make and model, the most important thing is the miles. But maybe, in the case of people, what matters just as much is the landscapes gone through, the roads taken, the milestones passed.

In the end, isn't that really the beauty of life—that you're living it and you're turning out fine. Best of all, you have something to show for it.

I am Hot

I am a 50-year-old woman
And sometimes I am hot.

Really hot.

Sometimes I look good.
Sometimes I feel good.
Sometimes I feel good about how I look.

And sometimes I am just plain hot.
Sweating hot.

Flashes of hot that
Irritate me so that I am
Hot all over—
Even under my collar.

Can anyone see that I am hot
When I am this hot?

Are there any cute guys out there—
I mean really hot guys—
Who notice how hot I am?

These hot flashes,
They really burn me up.

Pithy Cakes

She's Got a Ticket to Ride

M y first album, bought with babysitting earnings in the late '70s, was The Best of the Carpenters. I wore that thing out. I remember all the lyrics from every song on that album, which came in handy when I found myself singing karaoke in Japan a few years back. Discovered I could do OK justice to Karen Carpenter's alto register.

One of the songs I recall was Ticket to Ride, which I didn't realize at the time was originally a Beatles tune. It's about being left behind by someone with a "ticket to ride." Or, so the story goes, it could also be about getting a ticket to Ryde, a city not far from Lennon and McCartney where young girls were known to go if they "got in trouble." *I think I'm gonna be sad, I think it's today, yeah* | *The girl that's driving me mad is going away…She's got a ticket to ride, but she don't care.* I find it fascinating how that little shift in spelling can make such a big difference in perspective.

Turns out there's a popular board game by the same name, Ticket to Ride, which I recently played with my sons. It's about getting across the country by building a train network, with your destinations determined by the fate of the cards. The longer the journey, the more it's worth in the end. Now ain't that just like life?

A particularly long route will take you all the way to Vancouver, way in the top-left corner, and perhaps across all the states to somewhere like Little Rock. Here's the thing about Vancouver: right at the beginning of that route, there are two hops that only require one train car each. Piece of cake to cross that, unlike the runs that require as many as five cars in one throw.

But if you stake your claim early by filling in that uppermost one-car section—which can be any color, by far the easiest to do!—someone can easily block you by just laying down a single, any-color car in that next one-car slot. At that point, you are stuck with lots of four and five-car workaround routes that will take you forever to cross.

So we are playing the game, and suddenly it dawns on me: I feel that's happened—in my life. I made a move at Vancouver, but then someone stepped in and blocked me. That sent me to the other side of the country to wind my way back, and yes, that meant laying down a couple extra five-car tracks.

Not only that, the longer you play, the more likely you are to run smack into other obstacles, often from players who are only going about their business and not intentionally trying to shut you out. So yeah, that's happened too.

Board games work because they offer such an interesting parallel to real life. Think *Life*, *Monopoly* and *Operation*. But as with all analogies, they eventually fall apart. In the case of games, the biggest difference is the end. In games, there is one, and someone always wins. Which of course means someone else loses.

Thankfully, life, while much like a game, has infinite possibilities for how things turn out. And it never really ends. (Let's not get all metaphysical here about death—because even that ending is really yet another beginning. But let's move on.) So this is good news for me. It means I have all the time in the world to get to Vancouver. I just may have to get there another way. Hey, maybe you can help me. Do you know the way to San Jose?

Greetings

Hawaiians know
That every person living
Will breathe their final breath
And whisper Ha.

Ha, then, is
The common bond we share—
The breath of life
That ties us to each other.

Their day begins at sundown,
Facing west,
As the sun slips gently into
The great ocean.

West, they call Alo,
For what is next.
Alo, too means
The most important thing.

When greeting one another
They acknowledge
Their common bond,
And not their differences.

Alo, they say,
What matters most, my friend,
Is we share the breath of life,
Which they call Ha.

Aloha.

Pithy Cakes

All the Way Back to the C-Prompt

A colleague of mine, back when I worked for a company that made banking software, once told me how the company's product didn't always perform as expected. In the middle of one particular sales demo, in front of a room full of people, she found herself, as she described it, Blown all the way back to the C-prompt. "My hiney-hole was puckered up tighter than this," she said, holding up her hand with the index finger curled into a little ball.

One thing I've noticed about computers is that they can, in about two minutes, take me all the way back to a childlike place of totally irrational behavior: impatient, frustrated, exasperated and downright angry. Yep, essentially a three-year old.

So what's going on here? How is it that I, a normally logical and rational adult with a decent amount of smarts, can come unglued so readily when a computer won't do right? I suspect it relates to one of my childhood-created strategies for survival: I have to figure everything out—myself.

I was the third child in a family destined to trudge through some serious shit on the road to happy destiny. The long and the short of it is that I was not spoken to much as a child. The world is a bit tricky to sort out as it is, but it can be downright frightening to make sense of on your own.

17

So when that little box-of-logic doesn't work right, I don't default to slowing down and getting curious. No, I tend to come unglued and lose my grounding. Like a lost and anxious child, I have found myself on the phone with the help desk, finding it hard to use my words. With my Helper-hat on, I ask myself, "How old do I feel right now?" To which I want to stick out my tongue. So there.

Recently, I found myself caught in a phone war between GoDaddy and Verizon, each offering their logical explanations for why the problem with my website must lie with the other service. I had to coach myself to breathe, reminding myself that they were there to help. If I could just stay rational and sane, they were going to help me get through this. And eventually they did.

Today, I spend enough time *not* in that immature child-place, to recognize it when I find myself there. Much of life, in fact, is about learning to come out of these trance-like states that we snap into so fast, when something unexpectedly blows us all the way back to the C-prompt.

This poem is about chillaxing with Charlie and Jackson, ages 15 and 13.

Anchors Away

My anchor's too big for my boat*
So all I can do now is float.
   I paddle and splash
    But I can't move my ass.
I say, it's a hell of a note.

My anchor will break into three,
When both boys push off and leave me.
   Their lives will sail better
    Through all kind of weather,
And I once again will drift free.

So for now I'll continue to play
The anchoring role every day.
   I'll pause and enjoy
    This sweet time with each boy,
And not rush these dear anchors away.

*First line inspired by Shel Silverstein's poem *Anchored*, from *A Light in the Attic*.

Pithy Cakes

Why Paul Bunyan was Not a Tragedy

I n my home town of Rice Lake, up there in the hinterlands of Northern Wisconsin, there is a little cabin-rental place, right on the lake, called the Paul Bunyan Resort. From the dock, you can almost see the Blue Hills in the distance, that low horizon of hazy, well, hills, that history says were once taller than the Rocky Mountains.

Up in that neck of the woods, you can't throw a quarter and not hit another lake. And where does local lore tell us all those lakes came from? The footsteps of Babe the Blue Ox, of course. You know, Paul's sidekick. When you're a kid, you don't realize that not everyone has five-foot-high snow banks at the end of their driveway, and folktales that are almost as tall, at least to a little kid, to explain the world they see.

The stories, it turns out, are only slightly less strange than the truth, which is that long ago the glaciers slid through that whole area, shaving down enormous mountains and leaving behind all those water-filled craters we call lakes. What is equally strange to me is that these tall tales were never told as tragedies.

I suspect this is because back then, no one had property with a nice view to worry about. No one, in fact, had nothing. We weren't there yet to call all that world-changing activity a problem. Today, though, we—humankind—are everywhere. And global warming (aside from the question of whether we're the cause of it or not) is looking like it may be a real problem—for us. For Pete's sake, they barely even have snow banks for kids to build forts in up in Rice Lake any more.

But as pointed out by Eugene Kennedy and Sara C. Charles, M.D in their book *On Becoming a Counselor*, "Problems never exist in a pure state; there are always human beings attached to them." Think about that.

The glaciers of old weren't really a problem. They just happened, and that part of the world has never been the same. But should those walls of ice come sliding down Main Street in Rice Lake today, big problem.

There is so much more transparency in the world today, we are bombarded daily with news of the Next Big Problem. The government is a mess. Or the banks and large corporations are really stinking it up big. These entities are comprised of people, so naturally, there are always going to be problems. But for me, personally, the only real problem is the way I'm being affected. More to the point, if I'm not the problem, there is no solution.

Take anything that you perceive to be a problem in your life, and think about it from this perspective. How is it really affecting you, and deeper yet, why? There isn't a problem in the world that exists in a pure state. There are just people trying to figure out how to get along in life. And sometimes we bump up against each other, creating Paul Bunyan-sized problems.

White Out

I'd hoped that he might turn into
    A keeper,
Who'd share his humor and his heart
    With me.
Instead I got this thing on
    Dry erase board,
A picture of some flowers
    And a "be."

He said he couldn't give me
    What I wanted,
A lifetime of the laughter
    We had shared.
He only had this simple print
    To offer,
A stinging sort of symbol
    That he cared.

23

So now I'm stuck with this dumb
   Dry erase board,
Ephemeral as snowflakes
   In the Spring,
Just begging to be smudged by my
   Own thumbprint,
Another mark from yet
   Another fling.

Quick, How Competitive are You?

H erbert Spencer first coined the phrase "survival of the fittest" after reading about that which Mr. Darwin called "natural selection." It's a bit ironic that after all these years, at least in the public lexicon, Darwin was the one to survive the struggle for notoriety.

In today's world, this live-to-win spirit permeates our society and drives people to measure up—or get eaten up. Perhaps Norm from *Cheers* said it best in one of his all-time-great one-liners: "It's a dog-eat-dog world Sammy, and I'm wearing Milkbone underwear."

The key takeaway seems to be this: people will do anything to survive—to win at life—and if you can't take care of yourself, you get eliminated. Ouch.

So where does this come from, this baseline belief that there's really not enough to go around? For one, the ego. As I explain in *Spilling the Script*, the ego is a fragment of the greater real you. If it uses its timely wisely, the ego will develop the ability to continually tap into that infinite, unitive source of wisdom, creativity and courage. More often, the ego feels it's all on its own, and to survive it has to win. Its common refrain is "See me, I'm better than you, love me for it."

The second source of this fight-for-life spirit is that wounded part of ourselves that got stuck holding onto painful childhood memories. When we were little, we fought like the devil against whatever traumatized us and made us somehow feel like we were less-than, not good enough, worthless. And we'll keep fighting to the death to make that not true. This time, we're going to win. And I don't care if I have take down everyone on the highway to prove it.

In the end, this tilting at windmills needs to be exposed and explored, so we can start to see a different, bigger perspective: that it's not "me versus the other" in life, it's "me and the other." It's not a limited universe in which only the fastest runners get the prize. In truth, it's an abundant universe and nothing—nothing—that anyone else has or achieves or does, in any way diminishes your opportunities for satisfaction, happiness or love.

So if this is the human condition—this running and competing as though our lives depended on it—then in reality, we're all in this race together. That dog in front of you is chasing whoever is in front of it. Next time, perhaps instead of biting back and going to the mat for the win, throw your pal a bone. Step up and consider that under all the fur that's flying, you're on the same side. The side of life. And eventually, we're all going to make it all the way home.

So there I am, in the paradise that is Hawaii, at a 10-day poetry retreat where once or more a day, we'd immerse in poetry dives. They began with this wonderful cellist laying down the most heavenly music by way of her electric cello. Then memorized poems would begin to spontaneously flow from the leader, as if a magic chanteuse had coaxed them from cobra. At some point, the energy in the room would erupt, and poetry bits would explode inside each of us, inspiring us to write. After, lying spent on the floor, we would gather ourselves back together, and share our poetic musings with each other. There was never any telling what might emerge from within.

Verses vs. Verses

Now the poetry is the doing,
A new playground where I can be
    Better or less than, again.

I can't express without a ruler to compare;
I can't enjoy
    Without a yardstick in my hand.

As if there were points given for words.

Low poet points, go straight to poet jail.
String them right,
    Get Double Jeopardy!

Less than, greater than,
It all adds up in the end.
    The scorecard is held in the reaction.

Next I'll need my own soundtrack to keep up.
Where can I get one of those?
    How else can I stress in paradise?

Pithy Cakes

Should I Stay or Should I Go Now?

E arly in my career, working in the maddening world of ad agencies—yes, I have always thought the title of the series Mad Men was an apt one—I was one to jump ship pretty readily, crossing a bridge to what I always hoped would be my New Dream Job. But then always, instead, within a year or so of landing in the new Land O'Dreams, nightmare scenarios would emerge again. And soon I would be ready to hit the road. Again.

Only once did I leave a job without a net, swinging out wide into six months of relatively lucrative freelance writing before settling back into the security (and paid benefits) of yet another full-time gig—on the corporate side. But one thing was for sure: in all that coming and going, I made it a point to never burn a bridge. Well, except for that one time. That door did sort of hit me on the ass on my way out.

The real mother of all bridges, I eventually came to realize, was to connect the dots *in me*, to start seeing my own part in the never-happy-ever endings. I was sitting in my living room one day, pained to the bone about my recurring nightmares of day jobs, when I had this epiphany: it must be me. And this thought gave me a glimmer of hope.

Maybe it wasn't just chance. Maybe it wasn't bad luck. There had to be something going on here. I mean, I had simply left too many jobs for greener pastures that turned out to be just as crappy as what I had left, for this to be a crazy-bad coincidence. There had to be some kind of explanation. And as they say in the rooms of AA, Wherever you go, there you are. I was the link.

Shortly after that, I was led to the pages and people of the Pathwork, and a wisdom that would open many doors in my understanding how I am the magnet repeatedly drawing painful experiences my way, and what to do about that. I had really needed to find—and to cross—that bridge.

That was also around the time I took a position at a new company—imagine that—that one year later I was ready to leave. But talking this through with my AA sponsor, she looked at me and said, "Maybe this time your work is to stay."

It would be fifteen years before I would move on from that company. I did continue to change positions with some frequency along the way, but I was now able to build a network of knowledge and connections, adding value with each move instead of starting over from scratch.

The website Hp Lyrikz offers this: "Sometimes you need to burn bridges to stop yourself from crossing them again." The hardest thing is to know which ones to burn, and which to cross. For me, the biggest bridge I needed to burn was the one inside me that led to the place that always said, Jump. Looking back, it has been the teachings from AA and the Guide that helped me bridge the disconnects within myself, and build new realities with easier, softer landings.

Traveling Light

Yes! Yes!
How many ways can I show you Yes!
I am ready. I am Yes.

I can do nothing other than this.
It is right. It is good. It is now.
Nothing needs to be explained.

Just Yes. I am ready. Let's go.

Into it. Whatever it is.
It knows, and it doesn't need me to know.
It just needs me to be ready and to say, Yes!

But wait, I want to know where we're going,
How we'll get there,
What to pack.

Really? Do you really need to know?
Your Yes is enough.
Pack that.

What's in Your Closet?

In his gripping, insightful memoir *Open*, Andre Agassi says, "What you feel doesn't matter in the end; it's what you do that makes you brave." In other words: you gotta feel the fear and do it anyways. But as the Guide points out, if you didn't have fear, you wouldn't need courage.

Let's face it though, we all have it—fear. So we all need it—courage. Fear, in fact, is a fundamental part of the human experience, part of the human-fallibility triumvirate of self-will, pride and fear. This is actually what makes us human. Because if we didn't have these faults to work on, we frankly wouldn't be here. We'd get to push on to the next sphere of experience where the black and white of dualistic existence gets left in the Earth-world dust. Personally, I am looking forward to that way more than to my next long vacation.

But as long as we're here, we've got more we have to face. And here's the kicker: the bogeyman is us. We are the ones with the fear, so we are what we are really running from. From our own inner demons.

It is said that FEAR is an acronym for Forget Everything And Run. You can actually take this a couple different ways. One would be: just get 'er done, which is often nicely shored up with a little liquid courage. If you cut off your feelings clean enough, well heck, you can push through just

33

about anything. And usually find yourself in a whole world of hurt, further wounded by this ready-fire-aim approach.

Another option is to tweak that phrase a bit and just Fuck Everything And Run. Isolation, procrastination, sabotage and laziness will shut down the machine and keep you hunkered down. But in the end, we are controlled by what we avoid, so this tactic is also not a winning strategy. Plus it fuels the fear, and as the Guide often reminds us, it's our fear of the fear that makes a bigger mountain than what we're actually afraid of. Boy, we're funny creatures.

One of the more pedestrian acronyms for FEAR is False Evidence Appearing Real. Boring maybe, but bingo, that's it. All fear, believe it or not, is an illusion. A really good one perhaps, but not real nonetheless. And until we painstakingly unravel the threads of wrong conclusions and misperceptions that wrap around our innards until they bunch us up in a ball of fear, we are in their grip.

If we peer closely enough, we can begin to see how we often hold onto our fears like a blankie, as if their presence is what we need to keep us safe. Without our fear, the monsters will come get us for sure. They assure us that our hypervigilance is needed and is what's keeping us safe. That may be the biggest lie they tell. What does it mean to be safe?

At the end of the day, every single fear is just a crazy shot in the dark at what we believe has the power to hurt us. It's when we face these little devils head on, that's what makes us brave.

Imagine if Dr. Seuss got together with Uncle Sam, griping about the shenanigans surrounding Obamacare, while sharing a bottle of wine. It might sound a little something like this.

Bold

Once, long ago, on the road of royal hardship,
We marched to find our freedom—liberty!
We strode and we rode and we railed and we sailed,
To this land of plenty far across the sea.

Framed in our armor and faced with our foes,
We saddled up to fight for what was right.
But down through the ages, as we've turned over the pages
Of our history, we've turned into this dark knight.

No more must we battle with another herd of cattle,
For now we wage the war on our own soil.
We've turned one another—our own sister or our brother,
Into enemies to slaughter up and boil.

The Red claims the right to entrench into the night,
And stop The Blue from crossing one more T.
While Blue pushes onward in a futile try at forward
That is stymied, stalled and stopped relentlessly.

But if we combine these two colors in one wine,
And drink a toast to what we used to be.
We'll see Red and Blue as the building blocks for birthing
A bold Purple worthy of the royal we.

Now is the hour to dig deep and find the power
To get along, get over and forgive.
For, what did we fight for, if not the right to rally
And discover a new way to be and live.

Do You Hear What I Hear?

B ack in the ad biz, I found it tough to get my head around the cost of a single ad insertion: $15,000 or more for a four-color spread. One time. For something as amazing as an industrial pump, no less. So would you rather buy this ad space, or a NEW CAR? My mind seizes.

Or how about the SomEEcard going around Facebook that says: What if we fully funded schools and made prisons make up their budget deficit with box tops and money from Target? Sure, it's funny and makes for a good sound bite, but it's also out of perspective. These aren't the options actually on the table.

Here's the kind of choice we really have available: Would you rather be right or happy? Take that in. Would you rather be normal or natural?

I once dated a therapist who would say something like this to his clients: It's normal to wake up tired after a fitful night of sleep, drinking a big jolt of coffee just to jump-start yourself, and grabbing a sugar-frosted doughnut from a drive-thru on your way to a job that you can barely stand and feel stuck in for the benefits. To stumble through your day like a zombie, looking forward to cracking a beer on the way to the couch where you will fall in a stupor after dinner, watching mindless TV that isn't even all that good. Only to stay up too late, finally trundling off to bed and another restless night's sleep. But it's not natural.

What—really—are our choices? And what are the things we are doing like sheep, part of a pattern that stopped serving us long ago, if it ever did. We still clean our plates to be part of a Clean Plate Club, treating our bodies like a better trash can than, well, a trash can. It wouldn't be right to throw this out—better to throw it down. Really?

Or this one: clean your plate, there are starving kids in China. I had a colleague from China who told me once, You know what we tell our kids? Enjoy your life, there are kids in America who have no clue. Really.

When we start to wake up, we start to become aware. It's like a little bit-o-me splinters off and, observing ourselves, says, Whoa. What is this about? It this what I really want? Is this what serves my highest good? Er, you're right—it probably doesn't sound like that right off the bat. But it does start to notice things a bit more.

You know what really wakes things up? Getting quiet. Meditation makes people crazy because they start to hear the truckload of traffic that is jammed up and honking in their brain. My journey to solitude started shortly after a minor car accident. Fenders repaired, I drove away from the body shop before realizing my radio had been fried. For four weeks, I waited for the replacement to arrive, all the while driving back and forth to work listening to…nothing.

In time, I started to really enjoy that space. I started to hear myself think, and I actually sorted a few things out. I found some peace in my day that I didn't know I had. And I survived the trip without Eye-in-the-Sky traffic and weather. Before that happened, I didn't know my car could be my sanctuary. I wasn't even aware that was a choice.

Spray

That spray,
That pesky ocean spray.
Damn, will that stain my pants?

Shit, I'm the kind of person
Who actually thought that.

That thought got thunk before
I could snatch it up by the
Scruff of its neck and tell it to
Knock it off.

You stupid fuck.

Goddamn it, that got by me too!
Oh hell, and so did that last one.

Who's running this show?
Me?
Or the asshole behind these words?

Pithy Cakes

Like a Wrecking Ball

G rowth may come in spurts, but more often than not, it also comes in swinging, like Miley Cyrus on top of that wrecking ball. She's a prime example of how the pendulum of growth, when it's ready to move on from one not-so-hot position, often flies out to the opposite extreme before finding the more realistic—and sane—middle way.

But just as it doesn't work to follow an off-to-the-left gutter ball with one on the right, and then hope to claim a strike, neither of the edges has much to do with reality.

In spiritual circles, this wall-to-wall waffling is known as living in duali-ty. And that is a key selling feature for why we come here to planet Earth. To have the chance to wake up from this wild and wily illusion. Our goal is to transcend it, not get shredded by it. To move from "either/or" toward the "both/and" land in the middle, where "less than perfect" and "good enough" get along. To do that, we have to start noticing when we're caught on an edge, riding on only one of the rails.

Over the years, I have taken the Myers-Briggs test several times. The first time, I felt I nearly failed it, since some of my metrics were a near-even split of the two seemingly opposite traits. How can you be both an introvert, I, and an extrovert, E? How can you both love data, S, and use your gut, or intuition, to make decisions, N? How can you be a thinker, T—always mulling and considering—and then be tuning into feelings, F, too?

The bigger question is: how can you not? The work of introspection takes you inward where you explore your inner landscape, so that once freed of the brambles and weeds you can step out more fully—and care-freely—into the world. The gathering of intel gives you grounding in the five-sensory world we live in, but you have to go further and tap into that greater un-seeable source of all wisdom, creativity and inspiration to break through into new territory. Before you compose a symphony, you practice your scales.

We have to use our noggin to sort out our own distorted ideas, then "bring reason to emotions," as the Guide encourages, re-educating our feeling side so it doesn't get mired in the muck of wrong thinking and the associated emotional reactions.

The last metric is where I have typically triggered the tilt alarm. Planning and organizing, J, are my thing. I have—rather judgmentally, true—always tagged the opposite, P, to Procrastination. But P is more than that. It's the ability to let go of plans and roll with life. To be spontaneous, in the moment. This past year for me has been a chance to work on developing some P. (Or as I have chuckled to myself: time to officially grow some P-ness.)

Being in the middle is not about being willy-nilly, but rather requires the ability to hang out in the grey area. More than that, it's the ability to stretch oneself across an entire spectrum of possibilities, until you are so flexible you can reach out and hold both ends. When you transcend duality, you shift into unity, a whole new plane on which you have the ability to hold opposites.

When Einstein said, "We can't solve problems by using the same kind of thinking we used when we created them," this is what he was talking about. (Don't you know, one of the biggest brains of our time, and today we'd call him a spiritual giant.) So the same guy who blew away all previous scientists *ever* with his powerful equations and unified field theory, also ushered in something that has the potential to wreck the whole world. Try to wrap your mind around that.

Color-Coordinated

Luscious, tawny brown,
Rich, nutty chocolate,
Color so deep you could swim in it.

Your decadent darkness,
Set off by the translucent
Vanilla of mine.

Creamy softness, sensual pinkness,
An exquisite pattern of lines.

The palettes blend,
The colors match.

This is not stripes with plaids,
And it's sure not black and white.

Pithy Cakes

Three R's Learned from the Hell of Online Dating

There is a powerful, humbling tradition in AA, where everyone starts their sharing by saying Hi, I'm so-and-so, and I'm an alcoholic. I remember one old-timer who used to like to fluff his intro up a bit: Hi, I'm so-and-so, and considering the alternative, I'm grateful to be a recovering alcoholic. Ah, perspective. Reminds me of what it's like to do online dating. It's downright terrific, when you consider the alternative.

Online dating offers an opportunity to meet people from other walks of life whom you simply weren't ever—no chance in Hell—going to bump into otherwise. This has its upsides and its downsides. It also gives a glimpse into seeing what you might be getting yourself in for.

It's riddled, however, with lots and lots of false positives. And quirks—and quirky folks—I can only begin to tell about. On OKCupid, for example, according to one user, statistics show a high correlation between meeting someone and using the word "whom" in your profile. So, he asks, Whom loves you, baby?

This site has also devised a genius system of letting you answer hundreds, if not thousands, of questions, with a fancy algorithm in the background divining friend from foe. In the end, the questions all shake out into a few basic categories: Raunchy, Ridiculous and Revealing.

The Raunchy are, of course, mostly questions about sex. Do you want your partner to be kinkier than you? Yes, No or Not Possible. There are milder and hotter questions in this group, and thankfully, Skip is always an option.

The most Ridiculous has got to be: In a certain light, wouldn't nuclear war be exciting? And yeah, I have only seen one guy who answered Yes. But there was one. Gleeps.

More useful are the Revealing questions. The trouble is, I'm not always certain what they're saying. For example, to Could you date someone who was really quiet? almost every single guy answers Yes. What does this mean? It almost feels like a collective plea to *Please, shut the hell up*. I suspect I am taking something way too personally here.

When asked Which would you rather be? Weird or Normal, these freaks of nature, er, I mean men, almost always say Weird. And yet this is my fundamental issue in dating—trying to find the one who isn't weird. It turns out, this is what they have been shooting for!

Would you prefer good things happened, or interesting things? More often than not, they are going for Good. I give up. Everything is always going to be a mix of good and bad, and if it's not interesting, it can't possible be good. Perhaps I'm overthinking things.

In the line 'Wherefore art thou Romeo?' what does 'wherefore' mean? Why? Where? Or my favorite answer: Who cares / WTF? There was one guy who dissected this in a long-winded comment, explaining why it isn't really quite correct to say either Why *or* Where. WTF.

This next one may have given me the biggest insight into the great divide between the sexes: Which superpower would you rather have? Flight or Invisibility. It is nearly unanimous: all guys want to fly. Having raised two boys, this makes perfect sense to me. I, on the other hand, would, of course, opt to be a fly on the wall. And then, when one guy did select Invisibility, guess how I reacted? I don't trust him—no one wants to go out with some kind of creeper.

It's a crazy puzzle, so in the end, why don't we all just do what we're accused of doing anyways—looking only at the pictures. Well because, if I see one more half-clad-selfie-in-a-bathroom-mirror, I'll scream. OK, it's true, years ago, cough, I posted one of those too, cough. But fully clothed, I'd like to add.

Lesson learned, I started to write a short blurb about that, with the catchy title *Myselfie in the Mirror*. It was pretty short: *Please, cover the hell up.* And yeah, I'm talking to you.

Pithy Cakes

Scribbled while taking it easy in Hawaii.

Who Comes Here?

I would hate to live
In a place
Like this.

Day after day
These orgasmic waves
Pulsating, pounding and groaning.

Bright fertile plants with
Phalluses hanging like bulls
About to drop seed.

Birds of all kinds
Chirping sweet nothings
To rouse me from lazy slumber.

Day after day,
Night after night.
It's a wonder anyone comes here at all.

Pithy Cakes

Run-of-the-Mill Or Rock Star

I was on a bus ride in Canada, heading to visit my company's manufacturing plant. Along the way, I witnessed the source of my Canadian colleagues' bone-deep national pride. We had hired a tour guide to make the trip more interesting, and he was giving us his best, cracking jokes and telling us history tidbits. Although I'm no better than the next guy at remembering jokes, for reasons I can't explain this one has stuck with me for 30 years:

If a flea flies east and a fly flies west, what time is it in Hong Kong? Flea past fly. Never gets old.

Twenty years after I heard that joke, my job took me to Asia numerous times, and along the way I came to see something else about this joke: it doesn't work. Asian languages don't contain the letter L, so when spoken, it is often replaced with the sound of the letter R. Think of the Chinese restaurant owners in *A Christmas Story* singing *Deck the halls with bows of horry, fa ra ra ra ra, ra ra ra ra.* (Just image how happy they would be to see me—Jill Loree—coming to say Hello.)

My gift in the language department, it turns out, is speaking English. (My ability to count halfway to ten in Spanish, French and Japanese does not wow in international circles.) My good fortune is that being from the

Midwest, I have a pretty good lack-of-accent. And the upper-Wisconsin lilt I once had, I have tried hard, with good success, to lose.

With some self-coaching, I also taught myself to slow down my rate of speech. I did this by practicing talking, more, slowly, out, loud, in, my, car, leaving a little gap in between words. Six months of a class to learn French taught me nothing more than it would really help if they could just separate out the words—even just a little—when they speak.

So when visiting colleagues in Asia, I was often given the task of talking with them when riding on trains. And you ride on trains a lot over there, especially in Japan. My job was to make conversation with my colleagues-now-friends, to help them practice their English. For them, I was someone they had a prayer of understanding.

Riding around Japan, I noticed that, despite my only-tall-blonde-for-a-hundred-kilometers status, I wasn't noticed. At all. I don't know how it could even be possible that I would be so not noticed. Because I so stuck out.

But then I went to China. And it was like I was a freakin' rock star. Walking through a manufacturing plant filled with hundreds of uniformly dressed workers, their eyes followed me wherever I went. And not just their eyes, they watched with their whole heads. Wide, expressive eyes that appeared to have known not a drop of oppression, would shine at me with curiosity.

So that begs the question: am I nothing, or am I everything? Isn't this just the conundrum, when we put our perception of ourselves outside ourselves. In one case, I'm a burnt-out bulb; in the other, I'm a megawatt light. Same me, probably even wearing the same outfit.

There is a book entitled *What You Think of Me is None of My Business*. I've never read it. I didn't need to. I got everything I needed from that title. I'm the one who gets to decide my true value. I have it in me to stand tall and speak my truth. No joke.

Before heading to Hawaii, I'd called ahead to confirm there were hair dryers in the rooms. Yes, there were. But I'd called the wrong place.

Good-Hair Goddess

The Goddess of my beauty has gone missing,
I haven't seen a glimpse of her all week.
I thought that I would find her in my room here,
Hiding in the cabinet made of teak.

You see, she lives inside of my blow dryer,
She breathes her hot air onto me in waves.
Without her I feel ugly as a scarecrow,
Her magic makes my flaxen hair behave.

She works together gently with my round brush,
Adding poof that compliments my style.
Followed by a whispering of hairspray,
This Goddess is what makes my fine hair smile.

So I must search more deeply to feel pretty,
Or maybe I should stop searching at all,
And see the simple truth of my own beauty,
Without the perfect hair of Barbie Doll.

Pithy Cakes

Transference, Dressed as Nothing-to-See-Here-Folks

I came out of college boggled by the idea of discrimination against women. I didn't even realize at first that I was the benefactor of a dwindling, mid-'80s hiring initiative called affirmative action. Ah, so then it wasn't just an odd coincidence that the only hires that summer at the large chemical company I started with were three other technically-degreed women in their mid-twenties. Hey, I was just happy it gave me some cool new friends to party with after hours in downtown Philly, where I now worked and lived.

When I came to realize the whole situation, the two points that would hang up in my head were this. One, how in the world did anyone think that women got some kind of preferential treatment? All through school, I had had to take the same tests as the boys, and we chicks didn't get some kind of sweetheart deal for our grading curve. (Imagine the confusion, thinking we were the favored ones?)

And two, what else was I supposed to have done? I had a good brain, and now I had a good degree, and so of course I would go to work like anyone else. What difference could it possibly make whether I was male or female? I had also read and followed John T. Molloy's *Dress for Success for Women*, so we all sort of even looked the same.

What I have since learned about transference and counter-transference could probably fill a small shoebox, as there is not really that much to tell. But the list of the number of times it ate my lunch could wallpaper a large room. Transference refers, in part, to a person's unconscious tendency to overlay residual reactions to one's parents (or other significant person in authority), onto everyone in a position of authority who later crosses their path. As I heard it said shortly after stepping into my first managerial position, you're now the one everyone bitches about at the dinner table every night.

Counter-transference is what happens when the one in authority has a similar response towards the people they manage. So basically, I'll see you— *and* raise you. So while affirmative action was designed to overcome the bias of the hiring process, really nothing protects women from triggering every single mother issue that all their male bosses have ever had. So fun.

As the Guide teaches, there really are no victims in this world— everything that happens has an internal component that is just getting outpictured, often in our workplace. And so it is that transference and counter-transference show up in nice opposing packages that lock people into tightly strung tension fields.

It's tempting to look downstream for "the real problem here," instead of up. After all, especially in the higher ranks, the women are still woefully outnumbered, and before they showed up, the men were working things out just fine. One more round of scotch, please.

In truth, we're all human, so there's plenty of finger pointing to go around. Everyone has their yet-unresolved issues. That's what makes this kind of challenging interaction is so hard to detect and unravel. It wears an invisibility cloak.

The critical thing about transference is simply to know this: it exists. We are all—everywhere we go—walking around in a bit of a trance, overlaying our history on every poor schmuck standing in front of us, then blaming them for the way they get under our skin. It just happens. But it can be unearthed if we look for it. And most important of all, it can be unwound. To do that, we all—men *and* women—need to roll up our sleeves and take some affirmative action.

Pithy Cakes

How I Wonder

I know so much, I know so little,
Life becomes a little riddle.
Learn from struggle, that's the plan,
Figure out what else I can.

Gazing at the bright night sky,
I see Dippers if I try.
Nothing more though can I see,
When I set my eyes to thee.

Had I learned Orion's Belt,
Think then how I might have felt.
Looking up, my wonder doubled,
Seeing maps for when I'm troubled.

Patterns right before my eyes,
I've not learned to recognize.
Let these diamonds twinkling bright,
Lead me through the darkest night.

For all I see is what I've learned,
My own journey, corners turned.
And as I open up some more,
I'll see what was there before.

Pithy Cakes

Hanging, Like a Mobile, in the Balance

There's a school of thought that says if you spend all your time working on your weaknesses, in the end, at best, you'll come up average. Just like everybody else. But if you focus on your strengths, now that is the ticket to becoming truly exceptional. I follow the logic. The only snag is the way this can rip a soul apart.

Uneven development tears your inner pavement up, scuttling hope of ever relaxing into the peace that surpasses all understanding. That doesn't mean we water down our gifts. Nor does it mean we don't have skills. Cuz, yeah, I got some skillz.

But to continually play to our strengths—taking whatever works and working it harder—while leaving the lagging aspects to languish, is a sure-fire formula for inner strife. Worse, those were the parts we were hoping to pull front and center and polish, when we were making travel plans to come to planet Earth.

Balance has been a buzzword for a while now. We promote work-life balance, is touted in the halls of HR. Or as the spiritual community might om, It's all about making the spirit-mind-body connection. And it's true, when we're out of balance, we're out of luck.

The Guide teaches that everything hinges on the delicate balance of these three *primo* qualities: courage, love and wisdom. We each have one that is our core strength, but we need to have all three humming in harmony if we hope to walk straight in the world.

When we get lopsided, we'll either resort to aggression, submission or withdrawal, depending on our dominant essence. And then, in an effort to not get busted for our evil ways, we'll attempt to shellac that behavior over with the color-coordinated covering: a Power mask, a Love mask or a Serenity mask. How dare you question my authority? or, C'mon, you know I didn't mean it—how can I make it up to you? or, What—are you talking to me?

Here's where things can get tricky. Because the biggest tragedy is that our defenses—and the masks that we use to hide them—sometimes sort of work. Or at least for a time. We really do rule over other people and make them quake. Or we really do suck-up in such a way that we succeed. Or we disconnect, check out and rise above it, doing whatever it takes to escape the mess.

So if what we're doing is working, we should do more of it, right? Or wait, if what we're doing is not working, maybe we just need to be doing it harder. Maybe it's just our mask that's falling off. And maybe if all those other sons-a-bitches would do right, I'd be fine. Ever think about that?

In truth, little of what we're doing, when we're being defended or operating from blame or undiscovered faults, has anything to do with the core of who we are. And that's the part we too often leave hanging, in the balance.

Fat Lip

Like a motorcycle tire
Catching the lip
On a road
Being stripped of its asphalt,

I too was caught
By the off-kilter warp
Of your uneven development.

Soothed, as by the low rumble
Of a deep inner current,
My soul relaxed to the
Rhythm of your ride,

Then smashed into reality
With each episode of oddness—
Like being with one so young
He can't yet dress himself.

Really?

Caught there, on that edge,
I veered and vacillated.

In the end
I hit the highway
And moved on.

Pithy Cakes

If I Could Talk to the Animals

W hen I was little, I was fascinated by Doctor Dolittle. Actually, what I loved was the pushmi-pullyu—"the Rarest Animal of All"—a llama-like animal with two upper bodies that literally went in two opposite directions. I could relate.

The Guide says we all have one of these inner splits going on: two opposing pains with equally opposite strategies we're using—fingers crossed—to save ourselves. Talk about damned if you do and damned if you don't.

They come in different flavors, these splits. And the cherry on top? They can never work. To help make this more clear, I'll show you mine. And let me just add that saying that feels like a miss-hit golf shot that jars your joints, all the way down the line. My split is about being seen.

This is how my split sounds: It's painful to be seen, and it's painful not to be seen. The way the deck gets stacked, one parent brings out one side of our split, and you guessed it, the other stomps all over the other.

Here's an idea of how this has shown up for me. First is the part about the pain of being seen. This is the laboratory in which I devised my cloaking device: my ability to stand in roomful of people and not get noticed. This is my ability to fly so low under the radar that I will evade your slings and arrows, and keep myself safe. Safe from what, you might ask? Oh, things like the fact that you hardly notice I'm there. Checkmate.

Then the second part is where I fear I am invisible, and what, for God's sake, does a girl have to do to get noticed around here? I remember one day in college, walking to campus in the probably-cold (seems like in every memory, the walk to the Eau Claire campus was really, really cold), when I realized I had forgotten to wear mascara. Inside, I sort of freaked. How would people be able to see me?

Sounds loony, right? Of course it was. And because it was so illogical, I pushed that thought down out of sight, and it would be years before it came all the way back to the surface. I had a similar response not long after the birth of my first son. I was working at an ad agency and had a hard time feeling like I fit in. I later realized there was this hazy notion in the back of my mind that if I lost all the baby-weight, they wouldn't see me at all.

Other splits might be about being heard, or not. Or perhaps it's about wanting to be wanted while, at the same time, fighting fiercely to claim one's independence. Whatever the details, our splits will show up in myriad ways, big and small, and feel like an inner unending battle with the power to both push us and pull us apart.

The real fantasy is in believing we can somehow make this work, and that trying harder will get us to where we want to go. We need to surface our split and see the reality about what drives us, so we can start walking straight in the world.

In the mid-90's, I was working as a copywriter at an ad agency where we did some pro bono work for Jimmy Carter's The Atlanta Project. This was a hands-on group that helped underprivileged people through individual volunteer efforts. I wrote this headline for their poster: Face-to-Face, One-on-One, Heart-to-Heart, Hand-in-Hand: The Atlanta Project works, one life at a time. *Twenty years later, that work inspired me to write this poem.*

Heart in Hand

Face-to-face we stand
      Staring into deep black holes
      Falling into limpid pools of self
   I open my soul to what
   I do not know.

One-on-one we walk
      To the huff of heavy footfalls
      That gently echo all the way to here
   Vulnerable at last
   Yet tentative at first.

Heart-to-heart we pause
      Still-wet wings are set a flutter
      Softly setting up a rhythmic beat
   Breathe me now awake
   Oh, hello.

Hand-in-hand we go
      Floating into the unknown
      Silent as a wing or a prayer
   Hold out your sweaty palm
   Here, take my heart.

Pithy Cakes

Girls Just Want to Have Fairness

When I was a senior, in 1980-81, I was captain of my high school's pom-pom squad. We were a team of 24 girls who regularly performed a new routine every Friday night for the boys' football and basketball games. A new routine every week. We worked our tails off.

Before that, I had been a cheerleader in eighth grade, where our squad was given the honor of working at high school gymnastics meets, holding up the little flip signs with the gymnasts' scores. I got to flash the perfect 10.0 score for an amazing vault. While wearing my cute cheerleading uniform, of course.

These meets were very popular—with the parents. But the rest of the school? Not so much. You wouldn't even know there was a rest-of-the-school. Next to no one attended Tuesday night gymnastic meets. Here's what used to chap my fanny: if the boys' football games were on Tuesday and the girls' gymnastic meets were on Friday, I'm pretty sure that might have changed the complexion of things. But moving on.

In the winter, in Northern Wisconsin, absolutely everything happens inside. So during basketball season, that meant a scramble for finding any time to get in the gym. On normal weekdays, we wedged ourselves into practicing in the theater lobby, or pushed all the tables back in the cafeteria.

But close to game time, we needed to put the whole squad together instead of practicing half of us at a time, due to space. For basketball games, we also had to visually mark our spots on the floor. We needed to get in the gym.

For that, we always drew the short straw, getting the 6:30-7:30 time slot. In the morning. More like the short end of the stick. (And even though I only walked two blocks to get there, it royally sucked at ten below.)

I recall one day, during the fall football season, when we were miraculously able to book the gym after school. The football team was practicing, of course, down on the field. And then suddenly the skies opened up, and it pours.

Next thing we know, it's pouring football players in the gym, all across the middle of our practice space. *Girls, get out. We now need the gym.* Talk about going zero-to-60 in under five seconds. We blew a fuse. Words were exchanged. We were not happy. But in the end, the boys got the space.

Next day, I'm sitting in class, and one-by-one, they start calling a list of all the names of the girls on my squad. *Please come to Mr. Olsen's room.* Uh oh. I think we're gonna get it.

Sure enough, for the next half hour, the coach sat there and essentially told us, Girls, you need to understand something. You (the pom-pom squad) are only here because of the boys. You need to know your place.

The whole previous decade had been a busy time in legislation over something called Title Nine. In short, in sports, just be fair to the girls. Title Nine, we needed you.

Word.

So many words to choose from.

Work with them,
Play with them,
　Roll them over my tongue.

Some are delicious,
Some are crappy,
　You know which ones you are.

Of all the things I own,
I own my words
　The most.

No way can I blame you
For the words
　I pick.

Once they clear my teeth and
Head for the open spaces
　Beyond my lips,

These words I hardly noticed,
Whether they are pearls or bombs,
　Are of me.

Pithy Cakes

A Family to Call My Own

One of the members in a spiritual group I belonged to once cracked, in the midst of the Holiday season: Christmas is a time when we leave our friends and loved ones, and go off to visit our families. Mazel tov.

Families are such a funny thing. The Guide offers that these are the people with whom we have the most karmic history to resolve. First mom and dad, followed by the sibs. But as we all know, we're not always tuned to the same wavelength. And it typically happens that in any family—in any group of people, actually—the Spirit World makes sure there's at least one person whose personal development is most assuredly going to rock the boat. Cue the cannons.

Over the course of four years of high school, I did a whole lot of theater—eight musicals and a handful of plays. Two musicals were in high school, two in community theater, and four at a two-week summer music clinic.

The clinic began with Sunday-evening auditions, sometime around the first weekend of August. The cast was posted early Monday morning, and by 9am we were off to the races. By the weekend, five full days of rehearsals were done, and we had a chance to regroup and chill out together on Saturday. Since many parts were played by multiple people, we had a dress rehearsal on Sunday, Monday and Tuesday for performances on

Wednesday, Thursday and Friday. And Friday night, we stayed up all night long. We were kids.

The hardest part of the whole deal happened Saturday morning. The bond you can form with 50-some-odd strangers by creating something special over such a short period of time is intense. And every time, when everybody left, my heart felt like it was being ripped to shreds. My new family all went back home.

A while back, I worked with a guy whose wedding colors sounded odd to me: red and black. And then he proudly admitted, he'd gone to the University of Georgia. (Go Dawgs!) He was honoring his family of choice by wearing their snappy colors, blending the home team into the family home. Even the red-car-driving guy I sold my house to in Atlanta admitted, yeah, UGA alum.

Both my sons joined fraternities at college and I wholeheartedly supported their steps to continue to form and re-create new families. Interestingly and more correctly, my oldest is actually in a sorority, since post-Title Nine, both the marching band fraternity and sorority are co-ed. I may never have a daughter, but my son's become a sister!

What's helpful to bear in mind is that there's a little monkey inside each of us, determined to sort something out with our family. So when we leave our family of origin and set off to find our fame and fortune—and maybe a shot at a more preferred handpicked family—there will always be aspects of the earlier version showing up.

The point is not to ditch the family structure. We need support and a tribe to call our own. But my own experiences validate the Guide's teaching about how we each have a compulsion to recreate childhood hurts—*so we can overcome them*—and these came to us wrapped in the trappings of our very first family.

Absolutely nothing tops a handwritten poem on Mother's Day.

My Mother

My mom is a perfect mother,
She's also nice to my brother.
She does a lot to keep me healthy,
And we are so very wealthy.

She can travel everywhere,
And she has time to spare.
Every day she's there for me,
When I'm standing by a tree.

– Charlie, age 8

Pithy Cakes

Where I'm From

I am from soccer balls and Kodak moments
From cell phones and gas guzzlers
I am from cockroaches climbing up the living room wall
From lush red roses outside my house
And thanksgiving in Wisconsin.

I am from blonde hair and freckles
I am from Jeff, Eileen, Alan, Grandpa and Grandma
I am from going to the Dollar Store, twice in one day
From competition and arguments.

I am from "leave your brother alone," and "knock it off"
I am from the fruit of the spirit
And the Fruit of the Loom
From Norway, the proud home of the Vikings
And Georgia, the proud home of the Peach.

I am from cold pizza and omelets for dinner
From the family at the Fourth of July parade,
Cold lemonade and BBQ
I am from picking blackberries in my Grandpa's lawn
And playing football in my Grandma's.

I am from the shelf by my father's bed
Stacked high with shoe boxes
An endless landslide of the happiest memories we have had,
Left for future generations to see
Pictures of my childhood.

– Jackson, age 13

Pithy Cakes

I Am

I am a free pterodactyl
I am fun and I soar with my beak held high
I play in the summer grass and swim through that chlorine-rich water
My friends are as close to me as my skin to my bones
I am a free pterodactyl

I wonder what fills the blind man's dream
I hear the hooves churn the mud of my imagination
I see a series of doors
Waiting to open, or maybe to be left closed
I pretend humans are alone
But I hear the horrors inflicted upon Earth's other tenants

I crave a crinkled bag of Stacy's Cinnamon Sugar Pita Chips
My throat is cooled by a cold ginger ale
I thrive on ham and frozen pizzas
If only Hidden Valley commercials told the truth
Vegetables are nasty

I worry that everything matters
I realize almost none of it does
I acknowledge the fact that school is important
But don't you touch my free time

I am from lying on the heat vent with a blanket
And putting the plunger on the cockroach
I am from "Why don't you make me?" and "It's my turn!"
I am from the land of the Game Cube and the original Gameboy
But Xbox is cool too

I've never expressed a fear of the unknown
I believe there is enough to fear in the known
I let my dreams fill my wings
I am a free pterodactyl

–Jackson, age 16

[Jackson, honey, I keep telling you, in the South they call them palmetto bugs, not cockroaches. Whole different animal. Love you, Mom.]

Talking Trash about Tolerance, Tricky Names

When the company I worked for bought a manufacturing plant in India, I added a whole other sub-continent to my possible wanderings. I want to go, said I. No you don't, said my Indian colleague. He was not a fan. Not sure he was such a fan of his new homeland though either. He quipped that the only difference between the US and India is that in India, the poor people are skinny. Doh!

Another colleague did make the journey and came back saying much of it really was a shithole, like people said. Traveling back to Mumbai, a day's journey from the plant site, he had a pile of trash in his car to dispose of. Not wanting to contribute further to the mess, he was committed to finding a trashcan, but none could be found.

Finally, with no other options, he approached a gas station owner and handed the pile of trash over to him. The man, without out a moment's thought, gave it a heave and tossed it back over his left shoulder. When in Rome....

In these different ways we have of making it through, lies the grit that gives us traction to do our work. No lesson has ever been learned without some sweat. The work is to tame the wild one inside us, maturing the parts that want the world to look a certain way.

One former manager used to champion the notion that the issue isn't so much about acceptance as about tolerance—our ability to agree to disagree. The ability to hold our tongue, to not lash out, to not always have our way, these are the things that grown-up folks are made of.

We think that we can't tolerate the other. But the thing we most can't tolerate is our own frustration. Frustration is a word that should always have a caboose—some bits at the tail to give it a more complete ending. That would be "of my will." Because the only thing that ever gets stepped on is our own will, which is always saying, in essence, My way or the highway.

Perhaps we need to update our inner software to a more human-compatible version: My will or the high will. So often, there is another way, because there is another will.

I was helping a new employee, who happened to be Indian, get his email signature set up one day, and I was flummoxed by his name. I couldn't get my wee Wisconsin brain to wrap around it. Gopalakrishnan. Blue screen of death. I had lots of Indian colleagues and had come to know many fewer-than-five-syllable names. But this one took the cake.

So I cranked up my will and decided to get my tongue on board. The ghost of Dr. Seuss appeared: *No sir, No sir, Mr. Go-sir. / That's too many notes to know, sir.* But by lunch, the rain in Spain was no longer in the plain.

Back in college, I did pretty well in my classes—nearly all A's and B's—getting a BS in Chemistry with a minor in Business. I got one D+, a summer class, Finance, taught by my only Indian professor. It was two months of "mee-she-fun" that I only later sorted out was "mutual funds." I missed most of his words and pretty much all of the content. But over time, as I have gotten to work with so many people from all over the globe, I've developed a bit of a gift for understanding accents. Back then, I knew only the Norwegian lilt of my own clan. Well, trash that. I know I can do better.

While visiting the island of Kona in Hawaii, I was impressed and inspired by the miles of rock walls built from lava rocks. I was also fortunate to learn a little from a native-Hawaiian spiritual teacher about their nondualistic attitude toward using their sacred rocks. Any speculation about what might happen when a mainlander joins in, is my own. (Please note, no Hawaiians were injured during the making of this poem.)

Between a Rock and a Hard Place

Hawaiians like to stack stones.
Every stone,
Tool or weapon?

I hit you on the head with one,
To shut you up
Or wake you up?

It's all in how I toss the stone;
It's all in how it hits you.

I build this wall
So we both know
My boundary.
Perhaps you'd like to help me?

This one, it's really heavy.
This stone, it's tough to set in place.

Sorry, I dropped it on your foot.
Again.

OK, now you're mad.

Screw you. I don't need your help.
I never liked you anyway.

See that wall?
Get out of here
And don't come past that wall again,
You hear?

I know it's a piece-of-shit wall.
You won't help me and now it's all falling down.

It's your fault.
You could have helped when I asked.

I didn't want to use the stones I could lift myself
I wanted you to do it.
I mean, I wanted you to help.

What's the use.
Let me pile up some pebbles.

I'll chuck them at you
Next time you try to
Come over my sorry wall,
Without even asking first.

Why do you always have to be
Such a jerk?

Seeing You Seeing Me

My first job out of college was in technical sales for a big chemical company. Thank God, training was included. Over the years, I've been through lots of different training courses, and I've noticed that there tends to be an underlying theme: therapy. Yes indeedy, the world's biggest monsters are actually trying hard to help fix this place, one science-nerd at a time.

So this first training experience broke the customer down into one of three varieties: auditory, kinesthetic or visual. Bottom line: figure out if they'd rather get a voice mail, a handshake or an email—aka, letter, back in the day. (Not sure I now think that's how whole thing really shakes out.)

Nonetheless, before you can figure out the customer, you have to sort your own self out. One of the many exercises we did was about figuring out our own personal values. (Yes, this happened at a chemical company.) In hindsight, it is rather pitiful to recall just how badly I wanted people to see my brain. Wisdom was the primary flag I was flying.

This dovetails nicely with what I have come to uncover about myself through my spiritual path. I am indeed a Reason type. One of my strategies for life is to try to figure everything out. (Yes, I ended up doing pretty well in sales.) One of my favorite managers at the last place I worked—

another chemical company, in fact—used to slap this quote from Oliver Wendell Holmes, Sr. on many-a-Powerpoint presentation: "I would not give a fig for the simplicity this side of complexity, but I would give my life for the simplicity on the other side of complexity." I delighted in this.

I have also come to know myself as ENTJ (though I've been scooting across the midpoint in recent years to ENFJ), which I learned about in the infamous Myers-Briggs training. Which is basically another way of breaking down everyone's mojo so you can have some hope of "getting" your weirdo-to-you colleagues. Behavior Styles is one more way to cut the deck. Long story short, I've come to see myself from a few different angles.

When I was going through a divorce some years ago, therapy showed up for me in the form of, well, actual therapy. In addition, there was a state-mandated, eight-hour class. I realized that, not unlike at work, this was an opportunity for people who might not otherwise be inclined, to take a whack at smoothing some jagged edges. I was all for it.

In one exercise, they held up all these different cartoon-like faces—what we'd call emojis today—and had us jot down which we felt were us. What were all the jumbled-up feelings inside? Lots of sad plus pissed off faces in that crowd. Plus some happy—for this was in there too.

Then they asked us to consider what faces our children would pick. You know, the kids' faces were not always a match for the parents'. Especially for the parts of us that were happy to be getting divorced. It's that type of perspective that helps us see the other more clearly. The more we realize we don't know everything, the more our curiosity pushes us to understand. I am heartened by how much I've learned that I don't know.

It's Pointless

My poems today are linear poems.
　　Logical words tagged to
　　　　Literal thoughts.

Story is still told.

Story about nothing,
　　Still wanting to be told.

Conclusion. Point. Ah-ha.

Wanting to get it.
　　Wanting to give it.
　　　　Wanting to get it right.

Figure it out,
　　Then fix it.

Maybe I don't get it.
　　Perhaps that's the point.

If I have one.
　　Maybe I don't.

Consider that this poem doesn't.
　　Maybe I'm getting it after all.

Pithy Cakes

At Cross Purposes

S ome years ago, I attended a five-day silent retreat in the foothills of the Blue Ridge Mountains. Tucked into a corner of the woods was a tiny circular sanctuary, a space so small it could barely hold ten people. Windows all the way around with stained glass on one side, meditation cushions on the hardwood floor, and a "fire pit" in the center for a candle and some incense. I snuck out there every chance I had.

Just below the stained glass window was an altar, a ledge really, holding various knick-knacky items. The largest in the center was a ceramic 10-inch-high Buddha. Off to the side, a six-inch-high stone Celtic cross.

I have no beef with Buddha, don't get me wrong. But once you really grok the truth about Jesus, as the Guide's teachings have allowed me to do, it just doesn't cut it to position Jesus as second-stringer. Since way before some meathead watching golf ever barked it, *Jesus, you the man.*

So I would move the cross to the middle, and the next time I returned, Buddha would be back. Back and forth we went, me and some mystery spiritual-but-not-religious switcher. In truth, Jesus has taken it on the chin in spiritual circles. He's gotten a bad rap from being in churches, and that is just a crying shame. Because he's the main architect of the plan to help us get all the way back to God. I did my best to put this story together in the online "Best Of" Q&A Collection at www.theguidespeaks.com.

My passion for a more front-and-center Jesus goes back to those days sitting there in the woods, longing to know these teachings but finding most spiritual seekers had thrown out the baby with the bathwater. But, I asked myself, What is it I really think I want to see? Some big ol' maudlin 50-foot cross towering over the retreat center campus?

In fact, a few years later, I was sitting in Hawaii at a poetry retreat, enjoying the charm of the teak and thatch-roofed buildings. And I couldn't imagine a how a dead Jesus hanging from a cross would work with that ambience. Actually I could. So irked, I wrote a pithy little poem about it.

But the cross, I opined to myself, is how he died—not how he lived. Surely we airy-fairy spiritual-saint-wannabes can come up with something better. And then my brother texted me a picture from the front deck of my parents' cabin. Had I, he asked, seen the Jesus tree? Across the lake, towering at the top of the pines, stood the most magnificent 50-foot cross you could ever hope to see.

Weird thing, our cabin was about the only place on the lake from which you could see it. Get a little off to the side, and plain old pine. A most wonderful freak of nature. And it made me pause: Jesus, are you talking to me?

For the next several years, each time I spent a week at the cabin, I sat and marveled at that tree. And then I learned what the Guide said in the Q&As about the cross. This symbol has endured for the past two millennia because it represents our twofold being—the way we are at cross-purposes within ourselves. We desire love, yet push it away.

The two bars, one horizontal and one vertical, are the opposites in us that can be brought into harmony so we, as whole people, can resurrect ourselves. We can overcome our own pain and suffering, as Jesus demonstrated. He doesn't need us to *believe*; he just wants us to do this work.

We get to claim victory when we stop living self-centered lives and realize that we are all part of a greater whole. Funny, sounds like something Buddha might have said.

Pithy Cakes

Hanging, Out.

I'm hanging out at a Buddhist Retreat Center,
Little fat-guy statues here and there,
One sporting this dopey Buddha grin.

What if this was a Christian Retreat Center
With a dead guy hanging on crosses everywhere.

Good God, who'd want to hang out in a place like that?

Pithy Cakes

1000? Piece of Cake

When the VP of the company I worked for had open-heart surgery, our big-hearted colleagues in Japan got busy folding. Soon, along came 1000 origami paper cranes, a symbol of their warm wishes for his smooth recovery.

Like doing a 1000-piece jigsaw puzzle with your family, the joy is in the simple coming together. And isn't it true with puzzles that all the pieces matter the same, until one piece has gone missing on the floor? We're all good, until someone's not so good. Then hearts open wide and we feel the size of the cloth that holds us.

My own heart was busted open in 1997 when my 18-year-old niece Sarah died in a car accident. I remember sitting in my parents' kitchen the morning of her funeral, eight years sober, saying to myself, Her spirit has gone to heaven and I have no idea what that means. And I really wanted to know what that means. That prayer was like a depth charge that made a dent. Two months later, I discovered the teachings of the Guide.

I've referenced his teachings many times in this book. So who is he? It really doesn't matter. Because if what he said doesn't make sense to you, you shouldn't buy it. You are welcome—and from me to you, strongly en-couraged—to read his thousands of pages of teachings free online. Or, if you'd prefer, I have boiled their essence down into a book called *Spilling the Script: An Intense Guide to Self-Knowing*. You can find links to all-things-Guide on my website: www.phoenesse.com

Bottom line, we all have work to do, and we can either do it now or do it later. Regardless how many lifetimes you think we get, this is the only one we have right now. We should really try to get our money's worth. The Guide's teachings point the way to unwinding the twisted wiring in ourselves. This is not as easy as one might think. But if we're hoping to cheat corners and find a shortcut, we'll continue to short circuit our lives and in the process shortchange ourselves.

Like a smart lawyer who can effectively argue both sides of a case, we need to become more curious, be willing to take some risks. The hunt for truth is enlivening and expanding. It can feel like one of those moments in Tetris when four rows—bam—drop out at a time. New space opens up.

I was five or six when my dad put together a scavenger hunt for my birthday party. I broke into tears when I realized the list included a white feather. *Where in the world would a kid get one of those?* Well, we lived in a tiny town with one main employer: the turkey factory. And the trucks drove back and forth past our house all day. So good chance there were a few at the end of the driveway.

This reminds me of the way we tend to wear blinders, and then run around crying *The world is stacked against me!* But when we let go of the stories that make us feel like victims, we find long-lost parts of ourselves and can fill in our personal puzzles.

Suddenly, like at my party, new realities open up and there are 1000 white birds passing by, each one seeming to say, Come sit, all is well—here, have your cake, and eat it too.

Pithy Cakes

About the Author

A neatnik with a ready sense of humor, Jill Loree's first job as a root-beer-stand carhop in Northern Wisconsin was an early sign that things could only get better.

She would go on to throw pizzas and bartend while in college, before discovering that the sweet spot of her 30-year sales-and-marketing career would be in business-to-business advertising. A true Gemini with a degree in Chemistry and a flair for writing, she enjoys the challenge of thinking creatively about scientific topics. Her brain fires on both the left and right sides.

That said, her real passion in life has been her spiritual path. Raised in the Lutheran faith, she became a more deeply spiritual person in the rooms of AA, a spiritual recovery program, starting in 1989. In 1997, she was introduced to the wisdom of the Pathwork, which she describes as "having walked through the doorway of a fourth step and found the whole library."

She completed four years of Pathwork Helpership training in 2007 followed by four years of apprenticing and discernment before stepping into her full Helpership in 2011. She has been a teacher in the Transformation Program offered at Sevenoaks Retreat Center in Madison, Virginia, operated by Mid-Atlantic Pathwork, where she also led marketing activities for over two years and served on the Board of Trustees.

In 2012, Jill completed four years of Kabbalah training in a course called the Soul's Journey, achieving certification for hands-on healing using the energies embodied in the tree of life.

Not bad for a former pom-pom squad captain who once played Dolly in *Hello Dolly!* She is now the proud mom to two adult children, Charlie and Jackson, who were born and raised in Atlanta. Having grown weary of borrowing other people's last names, Jill now happily uses her middle name as her last—it's pronounced la-REE. In her spare time, she enjoys reading, writing, yoga and hiking, especially in the mountains.

As she turns the corner onto the back nine in life, she has consciously decoupled from the corporate world and is now dedicating her life to writing and spiritual teaching.

Discover more from Jill Loree at www.phoenesse.com.

More | From Jill Loree

Spilling the Script
An Intense Guide to Self-Knowing

I n *Spilling the Script,* Jill Loree has boiled down the essence of the Guide's teachings into a clear and concise overview that effectively spills the beans on what keeps people from living their best life. She uncovers the way our hidden defenses work, revealing how our strategies for staying safe are now the very thing that blocks us from our true loving nature.

The Pathwork program for spiritual self-development is based on the wise and practical teachings that were given by a spirit entity known as the Guide, who was channeled through Eva Pierrakos over a period of 22 years. The 250 lectures, available free online at www.pathwork.org, together with thousands of Q&As available at www.theguidespeaks.org, create a vast body of material that is frankly hard to get one's arms around.

During her four years of training to become a Pathwork Helper, Jill Loree had the good fortune to be taught by many experienced Pathwork Helpers who had each gone through decades of in-depth explorations with the Guide's teachings. Through their organizing, boiling down and sharing of these concepts, she developed her own deep understanding of this profound material.

This book, then, is not an attempt to teach every lecture given by the Guide. Rather, it is Jill Loree's attempt to synthesize and re-tell what she was taught, pulling this together with what she has learned along the way. As such, it is a concentrated—or as the subtitle says, *intense*—guide for following the most direct path to self-knowing.

For those familiar with the Pathwork lectures, this book will help you frame the work of healing, providing perspective in understanding the greater arc of the path and how everything fits together. For people unfamiliar with Pathwork, this book can be a valuable resource for finding a doorway in, or gaining insights that can help deepen one's work on any chosen path of spiritual self-development.

Throughout the book, Jill Loree references related Pathwork lectures, and has also woven in many phrases and expressions from a spiritual recovery program and other great thought leaders. In addition, she has worked in many insights from Kabbalah, which Jill Loree also studied for four years as part of her own personal work of self-knowing.

May these words open many doors for you on your path to self-knowing. Available online in both ebook and printed formats.

"The truth is that love is the key to all life and the only safety there is. That is the great truth…Before this truth can be discovered, you need to discover where, within the depths and recesses of your being—not at first conscious to you—you violate this law of truth and love. And every single human being does."

– Pathwork Guide Q&A #161

More | From the Guide

The Guide Speaks
—The Complete Q&A Collection—

By Eva Pierrakos
With Jill Loree

In The Guide Speaks, Jill Loree opens up this fascinating collection of thousands of Q&As from the Pathwork Guide, all arranged alphabetically by topic. The website, **www.theguidespeaks.org**, includes a "Best Of" Collection in which hard-hitting questions are asked and answered about religion, Jesus Christ, the Bible, reincarnation, the Spirit World, death, prayer and meditation, and God, creating a beautiful new perspective on spirituality. May this light of truth help guide you on your path to self-knowing.

"There are so many questions you need to ask, personal and general ones. In the end they become one and the same. The lectures I am called upon to deliver are also answers to unspoken questions, questions that arise out of your inner yearning, searching and desires to know and to be in truth. They arise out of your willingness to find divine reality, whether this attitude exists on the conscious or unconscious level.

But there are other questions that need to be asked deliberately on the active, outer, conscious level in order to fulfill the law. For only when you knock can the door be opened; only when you ask can you be given. This is a law."

– The Pathwork Guide in Q&A #250

Made in the USA
Lexington, KY
15 October 2015